Kindness on a Budget

*A guide to uplifting and
inspiring others through daily
acts of kindness*

Suzie Abels

Kindness on a Budget
Copyright ©2015 Suzie Abels

ISBN 978-1506-900-29-2 PRINT
ISBN 978-1506-900-30-8 EBOOK

LCCN 2015951613

September 2015

Published and Distributed by
First Edition Design Publishing, Inc.
P.O. Box 20217, Sarasota, FL 34276-3217
www.firsteditiondesignpublishing.com

Acknowledgements

I dedicate this book to all of the people I have been so blessed and honored to meet and who have touched my life daily. My beloved husband, Peter, of 28 years and amazing three children; Zachary, Haley and Riley, who are the sunshine in my heart's soul.

To my family; Mom Rena, Dad Jerry, hero Uncle Mike, cousin Manny, step-father Cary, sister-in-law Amber, and nieces Ella, Nova and Julia. My twin brother Jamie, who encouraged me to write this book and spreads kindness in volumes day-in and day-out effortlessly. To my dear friends, too many to name, thank you for your friendship, love and support on this amazing journey. To my editor, Anastasia, for her kindness, grace and skills.

Lastly, my beloved spiritual teacher Yogi Bhajan, who told me, as a young woman in my 20s, that I indeed had the most generous heart he had ever met, aside from his. To my dearest "Bluey", thank you for being a mirror, a light, and pushing me to go beyond my comfort zone and being a dear-dear spiritual sister and soulful warrior.

Introduction

You may be wondering why I wrote this book. Truth be told, I am no different than you – I face good and bad days, successes and failures. If nothing else, my 50 years on this earth have taught me the value of kindness. This book chronicles my experience spreading kindness, love and a dose of magic along life's many roads, on a modest budget. It is my heartfelt belief that these vignettes can inspire everyday selflessness and a contagion of small acts of kindness

ACTION 1
Hair

For those who know me, I am a simple woman who prefers ponytails and free flying hair. Since my Mom is taking my husband and I on a wonderful trip, I make an effort to get my hair properly colored and blow-dried. It takes a lot for me to commit to 90 minutes of "beauty regime" and the expense. I quickly remember it is Easter Sunday and with twelve minutes till my appointment, I jog to Ralphs - a few stores over and look for a tulip plant. I recall my hair stylist telling me she likes pinks and purples and purchase a deep purple pretty tulip plant and run to be on time.

As I approach my usual chair, she says "For me?" and I say, "Yes, Happy Easter!" She hugs me like a child hugs his parent upon receiving Easter candies. We sit, talk and laugh, and at the end of my 90 minute appointment I am grateful for how nice my hair looks and feels. I have no affinity for hair so I super appreciate her skill. As I am paying I notice how tired she looks, yet so kind. I hugged her again and tell her "Everything will be okay." Life as a single parent and full time worker isn't easy and she is a very good person and skilled hairstylist.

Total Cost: $8.17

Total Time: 90 minutes

Total Value: Priceless. The plant and my words uplifted her spirits and made her feel appreciated.

ACTION 2
Strawberries

It is nearing 10 AM and I am aware I need shorts and shirts for my Maui trip next week and head down University and Jeffrey for Kohl's. As I am in traffic, I see the large open field and 15 or so workers bent over picking what looks like vegetables. Tears fill my eyes and I detour from my original plan to Kohl's to the nearest store - CVS Pharmacy. I purchase water and assorted cookies and head back to bring the much needed drinks to the migrant workers.

As I approach I see there is the ending of a bike race for "The Cure" with police cars at the exit. I park behind the police vehicle and ask the two officers if I can spend five minutes dropping water off to the field workers. They say "Yes" and ask why: I say "It is hot and I really care." They tell me to take my time and I lift the 12 water bottles and bags of cookies through the long and narrow field. I quickly realize I wish to personally hand waters out and start walking down the discarded strawberry aisle. My new brightly colored neon Nikes squish with each step and I mindfully am careful not to twist my ankle as I am ankle deep in mud and strawberries. After several trips to get more water the workers approach me to collect it so they can pass it out. I look into their tanned skin and heads wrapped in scarves or baseball caps and could see their hard work and sacrifice! Perhaps, for their families, nonetheless, does not matter to me their reason! I see their goodness and tears fill my eyes.

Total Cost: $7.99
Total Time: 25 minutes
Total Value: Immeasurable. When we are blessed to see another fellow human being in some form of duress, in this case, the hot afternoon sun glaring down on them, we must do our very best in some way to help them. My hope and prayer is that these hard working people were refreshed and revived for some time.

ACTION 3

Airplanes

I had a strong intuition that something about today's flight would be challenging. In fact, I was telling my twin brother about it, to which his response was that it would be fine. We got through LAX security very quickly, which was a relief as it was Spring break for many schools in Southern California. My Mom and Peter were in the gift shop, and I sat quietly meditating in the waiting area. I always prayed and meditated daily and said a prayer for safe travels that covered both myself and those aboard the aircraft when flying. As I scanned the room it seemed like a quiet group of families with young kids and some newlyweds.

Once we were in our assigned seats, I was aware how cramped and hot it felt. It was 82° outside, yet in the plane it felt much warmer in the mid-day sun. Fairly quickly the passengers got to their seats and most closed their windows to keep it cooler. Parents buckled their young children in and the stewardesses went over the safety instructions. Soon I could hear several people telling the stewardesses they were hot and feeing in need of water. One father said his son felt ill.

After 45 minutes of waiting on the runway the pilot explained they soon would resolve the issue which was redistributing the weight of the baggage. I immediately could feel we would be going nowhere quickly, and my Mom, who has travelled to 26 countries, agreed. The plane was extremely hot and airless. I heard the younger stewardess saying it would cool down as soon as we took off. One hour into our delay, I sure wished I were in a short sleeve T-shirt and shorts. I dressed nicely as I wanted to feel like I was embarking on an adventure, and I always wore my black yoga pants and tees. I got cold water for my Mom and husband and quickly scanned the plane.

As hot as I was, I knew I would do best helping. As I stood in the aisle a woman asked me if I could show her child how to properly latch the bathroom door. She was already antsy and in the aisle, so I said I would do so. After guiding the 6-7 year old to her Mom, I went to the rear galley. I told the head stewardess I would be of help to her and in fact in any emergency, I was in seat 28C. I saw her quickly filling cups with ice water and to speed the process up, tossing empty bottles in the corner galley. I asked her for a garbage bag and as our eyes locked, I said she could count on me. The young boy and his Dad appeared, and I recommended Sprite or Coke to ease his nausea.

After over two hours on the airless plane, the pilot announced how sorry he was and we were ready for take-off after two passengers on stand-by had to depart the craft for weight restrictions.

Total Cost: 0

Total Time: 2 hours

Total Value: Priceless. Helping ease the comfort of my fellow passengers on the plane was of great value to me and hopefully eased their discomfort.

ACTION 4

Ohana

Being in Maui with Peter as my Mom's guests is a treat. The air is warm and balmy, everyone who walks by you says "Aloha" with a smile. Soon you begin to feel like there is a laid back vibe that far extends the resort and into the Hawaiian's lives. My Mom is a recent widow of seven months and would come to Maui with my Stepfather Cary for fifteen years. It is not that Cary was a beach person or sun worshiper but more my Mom's love of the land and its kind-hearted people.

On this night, my Mom made reservations to take her dear friend Greg and his family out for dinner. We were not sure if they would show up as we had all been unaware it was Easter. At 5:45 PM Greg and his boys aged 9 and 12 appeared at the restaurant. My Mom was clearly "Ohana" family and they happily and warmly embraced and began talking. Greg's wife was with her parents for Easter. The restaurant was booming with families and had spectacular views. Greg remarked they had not been to the beach in a year. I well understand him as it was easy to get busy and become muted by your own landscape.

As I excused myself for the ladies room, I saw a husband and a wife semi-blocking the path. He sat on the cement wall with his wife in a cumbersome looking wheelchair. At first, as I glanced her way, I felt such a high level of sadness, my chest hurt. I walked past and came back a few minutes later. I knelt down and said I had worn my small wood beaded bracelet while I meditated and prayed and if it was okay I would give it to her. She said yes, and I put it on her left wrist. I told her it would hopefully bring her peace and restored health, as that was my wish for her. I quickly left and wondered how many people walked past wheelchair bound people – was it out of fear, grief or just a way of blocking out their "story" of what happened? In any case, I was grateful I had stopped and perhaps shown her kindness and caring.

Total Cost: $5
Total Time: 2 minutes
Total Value: Priceless. Seeing another person's face brighten is a true gift to be the recipient of.

ACTION 5

Horizons

Again, I would like to remind you, I am not so different than you. I have good days and so-so days, yet I am always aware of my blessings. Being in Maui is a mixture of things: peaceful, beautiful, blissful, happy and at times tiring. They say Maui time to remind you the energy and sheer power of this island will lull you into a slow rhythm, hence, Maui time.

Today, after a nice breakfast I was heading to meet my Mom and Peter by the pool. When I saw a whale's tail breaching, I paused to see if it really was a whale - it was surreal, and as far away as I was the huge splash was undeniable as I could see it from the shore. I told several people about the sighting and two thirds saw the whales. One lady and her teenage son were from Russia. They were so happy to see the two Belugas. As I came to our chairs it struck me how often people see such magnificent things and don't eagerly share. I often wonder why and yet I am just happy to report I do so with a full and generous heart and I do believe it is worth the time to endure a bit of awkwardness when approaching strangers and risking looking foolish to gift the incredible sightings of whales.

Total Cost: 0
Total Time: 10 minutes
Total Value: Immeasurable. It simply feels good to be kind and share.

ACTION 6

Connection

After a great three mile morning fast paced walk along the beach path, I was really exhausted. It is amazing how the heat sneaks up on you and it really was worth it! Peter spoke with a young man and his girlfriend about why he was in an ankle brace and limping. Apparently, he jumped over a fence in flip-flops and badly sprained his ankle in pursuit of a Maui adventure. Later, when I saw him hobbling around, his each step looked so painful; I winced looking at him struggle. We were already done floating on our neon-orange and green rafts around the pool. I carried them over and asked if they would like them for the day - they looked at me at first like I was an alien. I smiled and said they would love floating and they said "Yes" in unison.

I really always hope and pray that in my lifetime it will be the norm one day to be super generous, giving, loving and kind and that in itself becomes the new norm. I saw the couple later when they brought back the rafts to our area and they were really glad they took them.

Total Cost: 0
Total Time: 1 minute
Total Value: Priceless, when a mother, seeing a young man relaxing in the pool and not grimacing in pain.

ACTION 7

Bathrooms

Everywhere I go, I always notice the cleanliness of the public bathrooms. Call it a pet-peeve of mine, but I like a pristine bathroom. When I am on the road, I am always happy to see a Chevron station as 95% of the time, my experience has been that they are very clean. Do not take this the wrong way; I am not referring to needing a fancy bathroom, just clean. How many times have you guys been to a restaurant or a hotel and there is a lady cleaning each stall? Even at airports, there are people serving the guests by drying the counters and re-filling toilet paper rolls and seat covers. It may not be an envied job, yet it is necessary.

On vacation in Maui, I was in a small bathroom at Whalers Cove. There was a 4ft 5" quiet woman in her mid-50s, tidying the bathroom. As I glanced around, I noticed it was immaculate. After washing my hands, she was standing outside, with her small cart of supplies. I reached into my backpack where I usually always have some small trinket and brought forth a small Ziploc bag. I knew immediately what I would give her. I said, "Excuse me; I was just wondering if it was okay if I gave you this pewter angel coin? I give them to people I meet who I appreciate and are doing a great job." Before she could answer, I placed the coin in her left child-sized hand, looked her in the eyes and said, "Thank you and good luck." No words needed as we looked kindly at each other and I walked down the stairway.

Total Cost: $2
Total Time: 2-3 minutes
Total Value: Priceless. Sharing, gratitude and appreciation with a woman keeping public bathrooms pristine, perhaps, in some way made her feel seen and of value.

ACTION 8

Shuttles

A tan skinned surfer looking dude with worker's hands and golden hair of sandy beaches drove us 30 minutes to a small town to meet the other hikers going to Haiku's rainforest. Eddie was maybe 35-40 and very knowledgeable about Hawaii. He told the six passengers the history of Maui and some of the smaller islands. As he spoke, I quickly got a sense that he loved living on Maui. He said he was surfing 30 years and was not famous, yet respected among the locals. He was attentive to our interests and a nice guy. Hawaiian music was playing in the car as he waited for the other van to arrive.

As we got ready to leave, I gave him a tip. He said in his eight years of driving people he had never received a tip. I said, "Well, I enjoyed learning about the island and rich history" and thanked him. He joked with Jeremy, who would be our driver and rainforest guide, to watch out for me - I would be trouble, and we both laughed. When someone does their job, yes they do get paid, however, giving a small tip or a gesture of gratitude does not take much. Our 30 minute ride was so much better with this one cool guy at the wheel.

It is easy to just side-step appreciation and I am asked often why tip or fill out a form of praise if they are getting compensated for their jobs. I can't tell you what is right for you. Yet my experience has shown me time and time again that when you put out your heart it comes back through just a simple act of kindness and gratitude. I have seen people I know begrudgingly tip or offer thanks and it does not work that way. If it is in your consciousness and heart to recognize someone, then do it, if not, the universe feels it.

Total Cost: $10
Total Time: 30 minutes
Total Value: Priceless. Acknowledging somebody who goes above and beyond their job's title and recognizing them creates contentment.

ACTION 9

Housekeeping

I am fortunate to be in a beautiful resort as my Mom's guest. I have clean white crispy sheets, many towels, pretty scented soaps and an ocean view room that defies the picturesque postcards that fill the gift shop. I can't help but notice the women who come from 8 AM to 4 PM and go mostly unnoticed cleaning the guest rooms.

The reason I mention this is to invite you to consider, would it take much time or even money to make someone's day? A smile, a snack from breakfast, $10 or a thank you note. I always travel with colored markers and paper and leave on the bathroom counter a note saying "Thank you very much for cleaning my room today, I appreciate it very much" with five dollars and a few candies, to sweeten the message.

Total Cost: $5.50
Total Time: 1 minute
Total Value: Priceless. An attitude of gratitude often breads appreciation.

ACTION 10

Maui

Sometimes I have found a few kind sentences mean more than any monetary gift. I met a young Hawaiian man whose entire family carves from the Koa plant magnificent artifacts from turtles to exquisite paddles. He told me he and his Dad hand-carved tusks and gorgeous Koa paddles. The pride he exuded while describing his love for carving warmed my heart's soul. I told him how much I valued his artistry and skill. I told him while I could not afford the $98 for the tusk hand carved treasures; I most certainly saw they were indeed worth what he charged. As I left his table, I saw him standing and admiring his items with a glimmer in his eyes.

Total Cost: 0

Total Time: 10 minutes

Total Value: Immeasurable. Somebody who works with their hands, generation to generation creating magnificent and artistic wood renderings is a gift in itself. Reflecting the beauty of their creation, perhaps may uplift their spirit.

ACTION 11

Feet

Returning from Maui on a crowded-snug aircraft, it is easy to understand why often people become uptight and unglued. As I surveyed the interior of our plane, I was amazed at how many people were on board. This particular flight had many, many small kids with parents busying themselves to keep them occupied. As I sank into my seat I was sure it would not be long till I was in a deep sleep. Then my seat was brought to life by little feet tapping, kicking, and pushing trying to get themselves cozy. As I observed my own response it was quite mindful: either I accepted I had a restless child kicking my seat and surrender to it or get upset and fight the current of my circumstances. I chose to take a very deep inhale and exhale peacefulness to surround me.

I am no different than you and was tired, hungry and cramped in a small seat. I simply chose to allow what was occurring not to disturb my rest. As I rummaged through my backpack, I got my crackers and refreshing lemon hand wipes. I turned to the Mom behind me and offered her some for her two children as I had plenty. She thanked me and said they forgot their wipes. She then said her daughter's chair was broken and she was sorry for all the movement.

As I looked at this young family in their 30s with two kids, maybe in first grade like my niece, I was struck by how simple it was to share and therefore unite with others. The kids said they had school in a few days, and I told them my youngest son was returning from London and going back to school Monday. I was also acutely aware that we are always given a choice as to how we respond in any given moment. While it would have been easy to get upset at being jarred from rest, I chose my own peace and to share my snacks.

Total Cost: $1
Total Time: 6-8 minutes
Total Value: Priceless. There is no dollar amount one can put on their own inner peace. I learned from a very dear friend, named Blue, that "the pause between the breath" is a tool that can transform the moment.

ACTION 12

Home

My son is nearly driving and at 5ft9 he towers over his mama. Yet, to me I treasure him like one would value hand spun silk from the Ming Dynasty or priceless rubies. He is simply my youngest child and yes, beloved son. When I make his bed each morning, I always smile thinking about his incredible heart of gold.

His room truly shows who he is: photography lines his walls that he took with pride, pictures of family, friends, sports cars and nature. If I could describe Riley, it would include *heart, light, magical*, and definitely include the word *kind*. As I write a note saying "Wherever you go and whatever you do, please know I am always with you in your heart," I carefully place his favorite colorful Mentos and open his window which breathes cold air into his warm room.

Leaving notes, a small trinket, gum for your kids takes little time or money. What really brought me to tears was when I was putting Riley's socks away and found all the notes I have left in a small folder. Tears of gratitude, somehow knowing one day he too will do the same for his kids.

Total Cost: 99c Mentos

Total Time: 6 minutes

Total Value: Priceless. The lessons and impact from the mother to her child, hopefully, stands the test of time and one day transfers to them as parent to their child. Love in all of its manifestations, I believe, teaches love.

ACTION 13

Secret Garden

At the end of a street is a driveway that winds upward leading to a parking lot with ten or so spots where I suppose people gather for their lunch breaks, a quick nap, a phone call, a smoke, etc. I stumbled upon this place with a view eight years ago. We were leasing a house in a gated community that my step-father insisted we lease: it was far too big, fancy and it seemed so strange to me that a guard had to let my friends enter when access by gate was simple.

In walking all around this new area over a few weeks, I walked my then young son (around eight) to his new friend at the end of a cul-de-sac. Many of the kids, including my own son, thought it was fun to slide down on cardboard or in my case scoot on my bottom down the cemented path. It led to this parking lot and I learned of it then. It seemed to me there were great views so one morning a very dear friend of mine met me there to meditate. It became a special and sacred place to meet. I soon learned from my friend, if we climbed through the shrubs and up some loose gravel, we could sit on a rock bed with beautiful views of sunrise and sunset. A small tree was there and soon I began to water it and on occasion I would leave a pretty rock or an encouraging note.

Over time, when my friend and I parted, it became still a place of peace and reflection for me. I had an idea one day when I was in my yard, what if I created a secret garden for the many people who sat there at lunch, mid-day and sunset, where they could read positive (anonymous) notes of inspiration? I slowly brought small and medium plants in pots from my own yard and stepping stones with messages like "dream," "hope," and "welcome." I seemed to mostly be able to time my comings and goings without being seen, as I wanted it to be anonymous notes of "you can make it" and "things can and will get better."

One day when I was watering and changing the note, a young couple in their early 20s approached me - they said they loved coming here and so many of their friends felt the peace and looked forward to the weekly messages tacked to the tree. It started out being strewn with trash, beer bottles, broke glass, etc. Once the secret garden began, the amount of debris lessened substantially. People can feel the presence of peace even if they do not yet embody that peace.

Over time, as I brought my own children there at sunsets, I began to see familiar faces. The age range was mostly 19-30 young adults on the hill, with my fifty year age group and older at picnic tables to read or have lunch. If I would go hiking in nature and find a heart shaped rock, I would bring it here. I had an idea to leave a small blank journal with pens and wrote: "Write your thoughts down." It was really amazing how quickly that first book filled up. The third book was half way through to completion; I looked at the happy garden and thought how wonderful it would be if schools or even colleges created these small gardens of love and peace and took turns maintaining them.

Over the blessed time of tending to this garden, I met some really nice people who would help me by watering and making sure no trash was left when I was away. One of the guys in his early twenties told me I had created a mini United Nations. People from Newport Beach, Dubai, Syria, India, Mexico, and Nigeria visited the garden. It took so little and helped so many feel a part of something, people would leave small rocks, heart-shaped stones and even notes of encouragement to each other: what a gift and blessing to have been able to create such a place.

People wrote of new found hope, inspiration and determination found on a rock near a tree. When bark went on sale, I created a pathway with it and enlisted the help of the couple and a man in his 50s.

Leave a note of hope whenever you can and plant a garden of love - you never know who it will impact, motivate, inspire and perhaps save.

Total Cost: bark, 3 bags for $10

Total Time: 35 minutes a week

Total Value: Immeasurable. Knowing that one person's life was inspired, uplifted or saved by sitting or reading a beautiful note or picking up a colorful rock, has meaning beyond time, price and reason.

ACTION 14

Donuts

Most people, I have found in my life, respond to appreciation and kindness. I needed to go to my neighborhood Mobil service station because we do not own a drill and my son's car pedals were being changed. I have known Mike, the manager, for years. He is very good at his job and treats his nine to five mechanics well. I asked if he could drill the new pedals and he said his worker would do it and just to give him a tip.

He has a hearing-impaired employee, who is very fast at his job. He reads lips so I slowed my speaking down as I can sometimes race my words. He drilled the pedals in five minutes and I tipped him well. I told him he was so fast and my son would be very happy. I went into the small mini-mart and bought donuts - I got chocolate and cinnamon crumbs and went to each of the five men and handed them two each.

What I always find interesting is the look of surprise as it seems to me sharing a donut and a smile is my second nature. I wish deep down in my heart's soul more people would see sharing as the new normal vs. sharing as not normal.

Total Cost: Donuts, $3.79 (tipped $10)
Total Time: 8- 10 minutes
Total Value: Immeasurable. 5 people working hard perhaps felt appreciated and hopefully their day was better as a result.

ACTION 15

Kitty Litter

I was picking up some fruit and muffins for my friend's arrival early the following day. I noticed a pretty lady in her late 50s in an electric shopping cart as she was handicapped. As I stood watching her unload for a moment, I left my small basket and quickly unloaded her items on the conveyor belt. She looked healthy, radiant and strong. As I got to the last item, kitty litter, I struggled to lift it even with my able body. After a few attempts I slung it on the checkout counter. I could not help but notice behind me a very strong looking man watching me struggle. I quietly retrieved my basket and checked out. I wonder why he did not help this lady clearly in need of support, yet I was grateful I did help. Kindness sometimes only requires that one pauses, observes and responds to a person, situation or both.

Total Cost: 0

Total Time: 3 minutes

Total Value: Priceless. I was left being even more aware of my healthy body and a tender heart.

ACTION 16

Vests

I had not been in my local Walgreens for a long time. Partly because I only have a third of my kids living at home and in part because I have been somewhat of a hermit. When I walked into the store towards the prints section I was immediately welcomed by an older man who works there full-time. I said "Hello," and he commented that it seemed a long time since he had seen me last. I saw his navy vest, pinstriped dress shirt and a tie and commented on how nice he looked. After ordering my copies of pictures I was happily greeted by a young man whom I knew by name, I asked if he was more rested these days and he smiled, "No." As I left the store, I realized I knew all the faces and stories the people who have worked there had shared with me.

I am sure there are so many regular customers, yet each person knew I had been gone a while. I wondered if others had paid attention to the details and stories of those friendly and hardworking people. I do, and I will continue to do so, simply because I care! Some acts of kindness just require your minimal time and engagement in the other person's life, so it is cost free, yet rich in rewards for both you and them.

Total Cost: 0
Total Time: 10 minutes
Total Value: Immeasurable. Genuine connection with another is mutually important.

ACTION 17

Space

So many times I go to my two local mail centers; one for speed and second to support my neighborhood business. There is a fairly quick turnover for small business here as the rent is high. At 15 my son has his driver's permit and likes driving me on errands, both for practice and then to sit in the parked car. This makes him feel like he is already 16.

I had not been to this mail center location in months. I was pleasantly surprised as I walked in to see pale green and white tables and the main table horizontally placed. I told the three young women in the front how nice the lime green looked. As I paid for my stamps I surveyed the store - my creative wheels started turning. I politely asked if I could offer them some ideas "free of charge" to make better use of the space. I explained that the way the tables and many racks of cards were placed, it blocked their visibility looking out, both, at customers as well as feeling the light of day. They agreed and soon a man in his early 30s appeared enthusiastically thanking me, while asking the girls to help him move the tables. I joked with him (partially to awaken him to his curt behavior with his employees, perhaps cultural?) that I would help him so long as he was nice and said thank you to the three girls. He agreed and immediately was more polite to them. After 8 -10 minutes, my son appeared just as I said, "He would be worried why I was taking so long." I finished painting with my imagination a new canvas for their store and was really happy how open and cheerful it now looked! I told them I had to go and the owner said "I love you!" He offered to take me for lunch next time and I said "No thank you" and my goodbyes.

Total Cost: 0
Total Time: 15 minutes
Total Value: Priceless.
1. Kindness to employees
2. Goodness begets goodness
3. Nice things happen
4. Treat others how you would like to be treated, the law of karma.

ACTION 18

Mother's Day

Mother's Day for me has always been a day to celebrate and honor my Mom. I have never really thought about someone else hosting it or going to a restaurant. I enjoy picking out the bright yellow sunshine plates mixed with butterfly napkins - it brings me joy to set up the table.

My Grandma Helena, also known as "Lala" loved lilacs so I will do my best to buy a small bunch. My two older kids are away at college, so Zach's snack plate and Haley's handmade green tile, she made at nine, will adorn the table. Riley is the last at home and we got his childhood favorite Madeleine cookies for him to eat. Play dough and coloring books with Haley's colored pencils mark the play area for Ella, my almost seven year old, dear sweet niece. Jelly beans and a card fill a small metal box that I decorated with my 17 year old niece's name. I do my best to always include everyone; it is just in my heart.

I walk back and forth through the kitchen and smile seeing my 23 year old's writing on my Mother's Day parcel, which is a book. My heart strings dance, yet ache for my older kids. I am not a saint, I have some off days too, yet what really nourishes and feeds my vast soul is being loving and kind to others.

Happy Mother's Day!

Total Cost: $10 for the box
Total Time: 40 minutes
Total Value: Priceless. Seeing the happiness in my young niece and teenage niece's eyes, as well as my Mom smile in remembrance of her Mother fills the room with palpable love.

ACTION 19

Believe

Running into CVS to check for travel size items for my daughter's upcoming study abroad program in nine days' time. I could not help but notice the lady by her small collection table wrapped in a blanket. It felt fairly warm out, low 70s at least. I paused and decided to go back to my car and write a note. I always have one or two colored sharpies on hand and a few blank index cards. I wrote "Things are going to get better soon! Believe" in red. I handed her the notecard and placed my only change, $1.20 in her tin box.

She read the note and said "Thank you, many blessings." I looked at her face and could see she had been through some very hard times for certain. I told her I really believed what I wrote - she said she did too. As I was checking out I bought her my kids' favorite Hershey's bar and quietly passed it to her. This time we just locked eyes and I felt such a deep compassion for her.

Total Cost: candy $1.00, donation $1.20, note 0

Total Time: 1-2 minutes

Total Value: Priceless, if in any way it helped left her spirits for hope. Funny thing is, I was having a rough morning and yet did not hesitate to extend kindness to her, which also lifted me up too.

ACTION 20

Pay it Forward

AMPM is my quick remedy for a dirty car. You drive through in less than ten minutes and voila', a clean car for $5.99. On this particular morning it was very crowded with workmen getting snacks and soda. As I approached the line the worker asked if I wanted to donate $1 to kids with leukemia, to which I answered "Yes." He also thanked me for my patience. He gave me two 50c off cola coupons and I thanked him. I looked at the burly guy behind me and noticed his large stash of snacks and two colas. I asked him if he would like my two coupons and he half-grinned yes. I do not often drink soda and it seemed an easy enough way to be kind to someone who clearly did drink soda.

Total Cost: $1 to feed the kids
Total Time: 8 minutes in line
Total Value: Priceless. I left happy and grateful as my patience was intact and the smile from the worker spoke volumes.

ACTION 21

The Rescue

Every day for many months a duck, I named Libbie, sits near the pool most of the day. Around 3-5pm "Freddie" appears and they usually swim a bit. Sometimes they come to the glass door and peck their beak which is funny because they seem to know me and I say "Hi". Last week it was lightly raining and when I peered outside I could not believe my eyes! Libbie was swimming in the pool with fluffy baby duckies! I grabbed my phone to video-tape this miracle to show my kids later.

When I came back out to throw out the trash it began suddenly pouring. I went to the pool and could not believe my eyes! The nine baby ducklings were trying to get out and were stuck. I immediately took my light jacket off, socks and shoes and was a moment from jumping in when Riley appeared. Riley is my teenage son and he is fiercely protective of me. He said there was no way he would let me go in the freezing-non-heated pool and we argued for a moment. I said I would not let the babies drown and he immediately stripped down to his boxer shorts.

Truth be told we were arguing about driving and I was keeping my distance. Every time we tried to get the ducks they would shriek and swim away. The mama duck was going crazy flying over us then going behind our iron fence. I turned to Libbie and said, "I will do my very best to save your babies, please stay calm," and miraculously, she did! We tried desperately to use the fun noodles and boogie boards to lead the babies out, but to no avail. Riley had an idea and ran into the dark and cob webbed storage room. He found a large blue plastic bin, emptied the toys, now some five years old. He yelled to get food. I grabbed bread and crackers and attempted to make a food trail out, which did not work. Next, as Riley went into the pool he was able to scoop one duckling out. I took a soup ladle and carefully placed the baby on the pebbles. It was shivering and I ran inside as per my son's orders and got every kitchen towel. I made a towel nest so they would hopefully warm up. As each baby was brought by my son to me I made sure not to touch it. I took a chance and laid down and blew hot air onto their shaking bodies. I told Riley to hurry or I feared they would die as it was cold, wet and they were so small. He ran in and out, back and forth with the heavy toy container and after 90 minutes, eight babies were on the pebbles - in their towel nest, me desperately breathing warm air into their little faces and bodies.

I could not find the ninth baby and searched everywhere for it. Riley and I went in the kitchen as the mother duck would not go near her babies with us outside. Miraculously, the eight fledglings began to drunkenly climb out of the towel nest and towards their mama. They followed her single file and out the side gate. Riley and I went out the front door, he in towels, me drenched in yoga pants and T-shirt. As they approached the curb I held my breath, two could not get up the curb so I ran, grabbed a jacket to lift them and off they waddled toward the bushes.

Riley commented, "See mama, this brought us together when we were arguing over driving," indeed it did. I sent him upstairs to shower and I quietly went back to the pool looking again for the ninth duck. I thought I saw the duck and I took a breath and went into the pool. Sadly, it was a big leaf. I checked the drains and simply could not find the baby duck. I truly was heartbroken and chilled to the bone as well. I went upstairs, took a hot shower and cried.

I was grateful to have been there to help, yet, emotional for the loss of duckling number nine. What also hit home for me was how kindness in the home is a learned and observed behavior. My son, who was so annoyed with me over his driving, raced instantly to my side to help the ducks.

I am so deeply blessed to have a kind and loving son

Total Cost: 0
Total Time: 90 minutes
Total Value: Priceless. My son and I saved 8/9 duckies, and we shared a deeply bonding experience together.

ACTION 22

Recovery

The day after the duck trauma, I texted Todd, my pool man to please come by to help me see if the last duck was in the drain. He came by midday and I dreaded his find. It was lightly raining and I told him about the previous day's events. He went to the pool pump and located the ninth duck. I did not want to look. He came back and told me the duck did not suffer. I cried out of relief and he put his weathered hand on my shoulder and said he was sorry. I looked up into his salt and peppered bearded face and saw such kindness. I asked him if I could make him a hot cocoa to go or coffee, and he said "water please." As I gathered one of my son's red Gatorades and water, I put two chocolate chip mini muffins in a cup. I gave $10 to Todd and said "thank you." The kind and loving way in which he recovered duck number nine really touched my heart.

Total Cost: $10
Total Time: 5 minutes
Total Value: Priceless. Kindness matters.

ACTION 23

Pool Day

My pool man is an interesting man, late 40s, hardworking and kind. He is always on time and when I am in the kitchen, I can see the pride and meticulousness of his method in cleaning both the pool and the hot tub. He truly seems to care about leaving the pool and the spa in pristine order and that he does. Most Thursdays when he arrives, I make it a point to go outside, greet him and bring him a drink and a snack.

Because we lease our home, if there is a significant issue we have to get the owner's approval. On one particular Thursday it was hot and I brought some ice popsicles and water. He paused to drink and said few people ever stop to talk, let alone bring refreshments. I said it was hot and I was thirsty so I assumed he would be too. I also told him that I appreciated his help keeping the pool so nice. He asked if he could tell me a story, and I said sure. He spoke lovingly of his wife and two kids and how he left his IT job that was so stressful to ensure he was around to watch his young kids grow-up. He shared his story of his grandfather's passing and how he worked so hard

45

and died a premature death, close to his very own age. He knew that would be his fate if he did not change. He lost a lot of weight, changed his eating habits, job and felt healthier and happier.

He shared he was going camping to Big Bear with his kids. I remembered I had some camping pads from my older son's college camping excursions. I brought one to him and he said he had some and thanked me. I see him no different than myself and would want to be comfortable while camping, so offering them was the least I could do.

Total Cost: 0
Total Time: 10 minutes
Total Value: Priceless. Hearing my pool man's moving story of his grandfather working to his death, is a reminder for all of us to slow down and enjoy the people around us before seeking wealth.

ACTION 24

Garbage

Where I live we have large trashcans: one for regular trash, one for recyclable items and one for yard trimmings. They are fairly large and are placed in front of the curb. Our trash day is Thursday. Being an early riser, I have quickly observed that by 6am trucks scour the neighborhood for discarded items - bikes, lamps, surf gear and more. I wondered if I could get my husband and son to lift the lamp and excess T.V. to the curb. The next morning as I was opening my blinds, I could see the big smile on a man's face as he lifted delicately our extra, yet in good condition, lamp and T.V.

My motto has always been much like Barney's "sharing is caring," so I no longer do garage sales, just place a note saying "Please take and enjoy these items." I feel like it is such a blessing to share what we as humans have in excess and as simple as it sounds, we sometimes need gentle reminders. Later that same morning as the large noisy recycle bin truck pulled up, I motioned with a water bottle and two otter pops - I think that purple dinosaur had it right – "sharing is caring."

Total Cost: 0

Total Time: 5 minutes

Total Value: Priceless. Sharing one's belongings that are no longer needed with another person and seeing the look of joy in their eyes is priceless.

ACTION 25

Mail

It is Friday and before going out of town for Spring break, I head to my small postal office near the college to mail my Dad an Easter chocolate bar and a card. I also mail my 6 year old niece her monthly "surprise" envelope. The parking lot is swamped as there is a gym, a yoga studio and Jack in the Box, that I am sure the college students frequent. This particular office is very compact with three small teller windows. I can feel the tension building as people in line seem rushed - many people get out of work early the Friday before Easter Sunday so I am not bothered, it is expected.

The older postal worker is sitting down while the others stand. His voice is noticeably louder and I can see he has either had a stroke or some palsy-related incident. He barks to people in line and yet it is his efficiency speaking and perhaps residual disability mimicking gruffness. As I approach, say hello and ask how his day is, he smiles "Good!" After paying for my two envelopes to be sent, he circles the receipt and asks if I will do a survey for the service I received. I say yes and take my pale blue sharpie to circle for my attention so I do not accidentally throw it away.

After our dinner and cleaning up I see the receipt. I fill the online survey which takes two to three minutes maximum. I cannot help but wonder how many people do the "positive" reviews. I smile and hope this hard-working gentleman will be acknowledged.

Total Cost: 0

Total Time: 2-3 minutes

Total Value: Immeasurable. Perhaps this hard-working older postal worker will feel appreciated and therefore acknowledged by his peers for his diligence and hard work.

ACTION 26

Apples

It was an ordinary Monday of sorts. I had just pulled into the Pavilions market, near where I live, for a moderate grocery shopping. Always in the back of my mind are my ideas of what joy I can spread on my small budget, so my happiness radar is on when I enter the store in search of little items to help brighten someone's day. As I approached the floral section I bee-lined for their clearance section and spotted silver and gold shiny pebbles. I weighed my options and thought I could carve a heart in dirt then fill the edges with these pebbles. Total investment $6.

As I followed my grocery list and made sure to get my husband, Peter, his apple snack slices for his mini work fridge, I smiled at picturing him place them neatly in his fridge. After paying for my groceries I smiled thinking about the shiny pebbles. As I began unloading eight or so small bags, I glanced up and saw left of my car an elderly gentleman sitting in the passenger seat with windows open and many small bandages on his face, likely a result of skin cancer. As I was about to close my trunk and return the shopping cart, I remembered the apple size snack bags. I gently approached the car and said "Excuse me sir, I just bought these apples for my husband who loves them, could I please offer you one?" his dear, kind face lit up and he said "sure." As I opened the small bag I reached in my back seat for a few tissues to use as napkins. As I said goodbye and returned the cart, tears welled up in my eyes. Not tears of pity, tears of love. I waved at the gentleman and he waved at me, and I drove home so grateful I was able to see him.

Love is boundless when we are able to see our loving connection to everyone and act on it in small, yet meaningful ways. After dropping off and putting away all my week's groceries I smiled at how much joy I had received that morning

Total Cost: $2.99
Total Time: 2 minutes
Total Value: Priceless. Feeling and seeing the impact of a small bag of sliced apples on an elderly gentlemen sitting in a warm car brought me tremendous joy as well as, hopefully, sustained him while sitting in the vehicle.

ACTION 27

Thin Mints

When my daughter, Haley, comes here for various breaks from college she usually likes me to go with her for manicures. Sometimes I get a pedicure which I find very relaxing, yet mostly just to enjoy our time together as special mother – daughter time. The Happy Nails Salon is located next to Target in an outdoor strip mall. As I approached the salon, I saw a table with Moms and their young kids selling Girl Scout cookies. As you probably have experienced, it is hard not to buy an item a child is selling with such pride and enthusiasm.

It brought me quickly back in time to walking in the neighborhoods with Haley with her Girls Scout sash that I still have, selling cookies from our green wagon. The two kids ran up to me before I was at their table and I bought the thin mints. Wow, I remember some 40+ years ago when I sold them and they were $1.25, now $5. I remember clearly now I would check-off my list for the "nice" neighbors and we as kids knew whose door not to knock on.

When we lived in Colorado for two years, it was cold, snowy and our blocks were very long. I remember how important it was to Haley as the "new kid" to sell a lot of cookies. She was seven and a half, and I went daily with her. Now as I am back to the present, I march in to the nail salon and hand the cookies to one of the ladies. She looks at me and says "For me?" I say, "Yes, enjoy, they are yummy!"

The small gesture of giving a $5 box of cookies lit this dear lady's face up. I recall thinking if I had more money in my wallet, I would have bought a few more to pass out to the large salon. In some ways, I am always reminded that the act of kindness or love is important no matter how small or large. The next time Haley was in town and I sat by her side for her pedicure, a lady approached us and said to Haley in limited English "Your Mom, is a very nice, kind lady." Haley reached for my left hand and said "Thank you, I know."

Total Cost: $5
Total Time: 3 minutes
Total Value: Immeasurable. Helping support eight to ten year old Brownies brings back happy memories shared long ago with my very own daughter.

ACTION 28

Grasshopper

Just before I sit down for my egg white soufflé for lunch, I remember I need to empty the pool filter. Part of living in a house that we lease is being very mindful of the nuances of the property, such as the pool that is surrounded by many Eucalyptus trees. The trees are truly regal and yes, magnificent, but not for the pool man or drain that fills up every two days with its leaves. Sometimes, I forget to pause and breathe before opening it, as I have had large dead-inflated mice, baby mice, rats, baby birds and many bees in our almost five years being stewards of the house and yard.

Today I forgot to pause and quickly opened the ivory plastic lid and yes, shrieked as a large insect was eye to eye with me and clinging to the side for life. I quickly scooped it in my hands knowing it might not make another plunge in the chlorinated water. I crouched down very low and breathed warm air on it as I saw it was wet. In a few moments it jumped and landed back in the pool! I sprang into ACTION and removed the lid as a rescue boat - it worked. The large grasshopper did a huge jump, this time toward the sunny shrubs. I am grateful I could help this regal friend of the garden!

Total Cost: 0
Total Time: 4 minutes
Total Value: Priceless. Nature carries profound wisdom, visually and energetically. I am grateful to have witnessed this delicate and beautiful insect eye to eye.

ACTION 29

Grass

Just ask yourself this next time it is a hot day and your gardener is mowing and blowing the debris on your property in the heat of the day: if you or your kids or loved ones are hot, thirsty and maybe even cranky, could they, your gardeners, be in need or wanting a drink? Nine out of ten times, my guess and life's experiences say yes.

Being kind or connected to others is as simple as that and yes, can be done by you, me, or anybody. So each Thursday, if and when I am home, I make it a point to gather three or four drinks, take a pretty napkin (which I usually buy in Target's clearance section) and put either a cookie or an ice-pop on it. I then go to each gardener and say thank you. It takes three to five minutes, costs little and yes Dear Ones, it means a lot and therefore matters.

Note: When I bring treats I never expect a thank you or anything in return. The opportunity to provide the action is a gift within itself.

Another important matter to me is showing my teenager this act of kindness and human connection. I always have him say hello and thank you to Cesar, Oscar and their crew.

Total Cost: 0
Total Time: 3-5 minutes
Total Value: Immeasurable. Hard working people should be recognized and appreciated. It is my blessing to be a mouth piece for the many that do not provide the appreciation as one would expect from humanity, with just a simple "thank you."

ACTION 30

Argyle

Standing in the supermarket, I noticed an elderly man in front of me in the line, perhaps 75-80 years in age. I noticed his pressed khaki slacks, clean slip-on loafers and sweet brown argyle vested sweater. His white hair was neat and tidily combed to the side. I suppose he noticed me glancing at him as we patiently waited for the large order in front of him to be completed. He had a twinkle in his eyes and told me "Hello." I said I liked his pretty sweater. He told me his wife of 60 years had recently died and she bought it for him. I could both feel his sorrow, loss and deep love for his deceased wife. I asked if he had kids or grandchildren nearby, and he said "Yes, two daughters and a son, many grandchildren." He was a mixture of elegance, grace, palpable heartache and yet very pleasant and alive. I told him I was sorry for his loss and how lucky he was to share so many decades of love with her.

As his groceries were almost all bagged up, he asked me if he could give me a hug. I said yes and we hugged warmly and tightly. I told him I loved him and kissed his weathered, yet soft cheek. He said "Thank you" and that I had made his entire day as he had been so lonely and sad as of late. As he left, I felt tears well up in my eyes and the checker said to me, "I wish more people were like you." It costs nothing and yet gives so much. She agreed.

Total Cost: 0
Total Time: 6 minutes
Total Value: Priceless. Listening to a lovely gentleman's tales of love and sorrow and sharing a heartfelt embrace made my day as well, and perhaps made him still feel relevant.

ACTION 31

Target

I must go into my neighborhood Target store many times a week, whether it is for a fast pizza for my son or some quick groceries or socks for my husband. The point is, I am quite familiar with the large store and can navigate it with ease and speed. On this particular Thursday, I was in search of a specific item and had forgotten my reading glasses so I was struggling to read the size and details on the small tag. I politely asked a lady I had often seen to please help me. She found the athletic shirt in minutes, and I thanked her and joked I was not yet used to needing reading glasses! She walked away and I finished up my small shopping list.

As I was paying and about to exit the store she asked me if I would please fill out the customer survey form online as she was one of many managers and it helped her. I asked her name, "Lisa," and said I would easily remember her name as my childhood best friend is Lisa. I left and went home.

In the afternoon, I saw the receipt and where she had circled the survey info and got my small

Google-chrome computer out: I am very much challenged with technology, so it took me many attempts to get the correct feedback page. I wrote my honest review and went about my afternoon. The one thing I did notice is how easy it would have been to simply throw out the receipt, and yet I had given my word and wanted to be in integrity and express my gratefulness for her help. I would have never found that exercise shirt without Lisa's help for certain.

A few weeks passed and on my many returns to the same Target, as I was exiting, Lisa appeared! She told me in all her many, many years as an employee and now manager she had never received a customer's positive feedback. She told me it was printed out by a general manager and displayed in their break-room/office. She said she brought it home to share with her husband and two young children. We locked eyes and I just simply hugged her and said, "I appreciate you." It took me perhaps ten minutes due to my technical challenges and cost me nothing. The image of her face when she told me of her pride is etched in my mind and heart.

I am no different than you, please remember, so perhaps next time you are in a shop, take time to say thank you or possibly fill out a customer survey. Thank you can and does cost nothing and can change a person's life.

Total Cost: 0

Total Time: 10 minutes

Total Value: Priceless. Recognizing another human being's hard work and efforts, perhaps, leads to them having more self-confidence and a feeling of pride. Please consider this next time you are in a large chain store.

ACTION 32

Lottery

I guess I see myself not too different than others, yet mostly, I have the ability to see the goodness in people. I was putting some gas in my car and had to go inside to use the Chevron Station's ladies bathroom. People who know me well would laugh as I always say the cleanest restrooms I have found in most cities is at the Chevron station.

I decided since it was not crowded to get some pretzels and my son's favorite Kiwi-Strawberry Snapple as a special treat. As I stood second in line a very tall man in perhaps his mid-30s stood behind me- he was wearing a navy bandana and had a tattoo of a tear on the side of his eye: I recall learning that was often a young gang member's reward as their initiation in certain gangs for a particularly unmentionable act.

Being as intuitively connected as I am I could feel his gentle, yet very large presence. I went to the cashier and decided to purchase a quick pick lottery ticket. After filling-up my car I saw the bandana clad man- I on most days myself wore a colorful bandana, yet today decided to let my hair breathe. I replaced the gas cap and turned to the man who was at the neighboring pump filling up a large truck with workman's tools with gas. I said "Hey, I heard there was a big lottery and I was wondering if I could give you my quick pick? My only wish is that if you win that you have many good times ahead." He looked me straight in the eyes and told me in his entire lifetime no one has ever done anything nice like that for him ever. This 6'2- 6'4 man had tears going down his face. I said, "Well, perhaps your luck is changing." We locked eyes or perhaps souls for a moment and I waved goodbye. I felt moved on so many levels and again felt so lucky and blessed for our meaningful encounter.

Total Cost: $1
Total Time: 2 minutes
Total Value: Immeasurable. One never knows the impact that one small gesture can have on transforming and impacting a person's life.

ACTION 33

Licorice

Ever since my family and I moved into our current neighborhood and house we have leased, my husband, kids and I have felt very aware of the beautiful landscape - trees, red tail hawks, rabbits, coyotes, butterflies that are at home in our residential, pretty area. We, like many people, went through some challenging times and have not owned our own house in a decade, yet, wherever we live, I make the garden very pretty with bright colors, pale hues and peaceful trinkets and wind chimes from our life together. When we moved in the corner house five years ago, I counted eight houses total in our pretty cul-de-sac.

I immediately introduced myself, husband and three kids and wrote down names and some details so I could remember the neighbors. I noticed no one really spoke or waved at each other in our small cozy block. I asked my daughter nearing 16 years old, to make me a flyer stating: *Join our neighbors for some snacks, fun and games. Please bring an outside game or snack. See you ALL there at the end of our cul-de-sac.* As I put a flyer with

Haley in each door or mail box, no one answered. I said "They will all come."

That Saturday I asked Haley, Zach and Riley to please help me put our eight foot fold-up table at the end corner. I then brought out our colored chalk, Riley brought a Frisbee and Zach carried the snacks. I put a plastic bright disposable red and white cloth and taped it down. Licorice in a tin, cookies and water bottles decorated our small table. I had Haley, who is artistic, write "Welcome" in chalk and also write "Please sign in" on the ground.

The kids and my husband said "Mama, people are not going to come;" I knew and believed they would and guess what? Soon the cul-de-sac became alive with families, couples, and dogs. People brought salads, fruit and home-baked items and most importantly they engaged and spent time with their neighbors, many said for the first time ever. It was a special day and I plan to set-up that same table this June and share laughter and fun with now two new households since that August day where laughter and licorice filled our cul-de-sac.

Total Cost: $10
Total Time: 2 hours
Total Value: Priceless. Uniting a cul-de-sac together has brought more laughter and joy on our small block. People now know each other's

names and look after one another. Please consider this small gesture in your own neighborhoods.

ACTION 34

Community

I have a new friend who lives in San Diego County. After knowing her two months when she moved with her incredible dog to a house that had two lower-level fields, I asked if I could spend many hours working on a project there. It was this really cool field that overlooked the lake; tired and very neglected. I, however, saw it as a meeting place for the community that seemed to be made up of families as well as older people.

I envisioned a group sitting in a circle and drumming, dancing, playing joyfully, talking to each other, while animals roamed. I asked my friend if all the discarded logs I had seen in the forest, from the downed trees, would be okay to take. She said "Yes, they wanted people to use them for firewood and such." I tried lifting one log and soon realized they were too heavy for me to carry one by one, and my car could not be left on the main small road.

I saw some teens the same age as my son in a golf cart and asked if they could help me for an hour or so and I would pay them. I told them of my plan to use the logs as seating around the square and I would then use rocks to secure them in the back. They happily hopped on their golf cart and grabbed another friend: I wanted them to place them and I would go get drinks and cookies. When I returned 25 minutes later they were very proud of their accomplishments and visibly tired. I thanked them and as a mother, requested they sit down and drink Gatorade and eat cookies and praised them for their hard work and creativity in the placement of the log seats.

Total Cost: $40

Total Time: 90 minutes

Total Value: Immeasurable. Creating a beautiful and welcoming space for a neighborhood and their families and friends to congregate is a worthwhile endeavor. As it turns out, tons of people indeed did gather at the circle; drumming, singing and eating, while children ran around in joy. Perhaps, you too, can create something in your own neighborhoods, bringing people together.

ACTION 35

Moving

My friend texted me that her elderly mother needed to move. I can only imagine how hard that is on a woman reaching 90. We have moved many times in our marriage: four times in L.A., two times in Colorado, five times in Orange County and not one time was it "easy." So I immediately started praying and meditating on how I could be of help. I located a small lower level detached house and sent off the information. I sure hope it works out.

One thing I know having a family member who is aging is that moving can be particularly challenging for a senior citizen. Even in the best circumstances it requests organization, money, effort, patience and time. I am no different than you; we are all capable to extend our loving kindness to each other at any time. It feels good to me to be of "service." Can you imagine if we all chipped in to support, uplift, encourage and inspire each other just because we cared and not wanting anything back? I am in! Are you?

Total Cost: 0

Total Time: 4-5 minutes internet search

Total Value: Immeasurable. Helping support someone who is in service to their elderly parent is a gift in itself. How many of you have aging parents or know of a friend in the same situation? I invite you to consider in which way you can be of loving support to them?

ACTION 36

Daughters

Visiting my daughter for the first time at college in Washington was very meaningful to me and to her. I wanted to give her ample "space" to get firmly rooted in her new environment some 1,000 miles from where she grew up. After seven and a half months, I was "invited" by my only daughter to come visit her, just me, "mama."

As I booked my flight and hotel I was aware of the fluttering in my heart. I speak daily to my daughter, and do my very best to be an example of a kind person in the details of how I live. Truth is, it comes naturally for me, just like some people are wired to be athletes or entrepreneurs. As I packed my luggage, I included positive note cards for her closest friends, shiny rocks with "Allow," "Discover," "Love," "Gratitude" and a bag of colorful jacks. As I entered the airport many hours early, I noticed how for the most part, I could feel the gratefulness of my blessed life. As a result, I was ushered into shorter lines, upgraded in seats, given excellent service by flight attendants, simply because I was kind and yes, appreciative.

As my daughter pulled into my hotel, tears filled my eyes. When did my sandy haired child grow up? Enthusiastically, we headed for her University with warm weather and warm hearts. Entering my daughter's single room, I saw all the love and sweetness in every detail: bright, flowered comforter with sea blue sheets we had picked out together, pictures of our family, friends on work boards neatly lining her wall with colored push pins and above her door.

Total Cost: 0
Total Time: 4 days
Total Value: Priceless. When your kids grow up and they ask you to come visit them at college, never ever hesitate, do not allow money or time to be a deterrent as the connections with one's children is truly a matter of the heart, and therefore priceless.

ACTION 37

A Rose

My daughter and I are very close, yet different in many ways. I tend to see the good in everyone and forgive the not so good. She is kind by nature, yet clings as many 20 year olds do to her past hurts. When we went Saturday night to watch a dance performance from her college, I went, yet was not at all prepared for what would unfold. We arrived at a beautiful church in downtown Tacoma, Washington, that was in many ways beautiful with high detailed ceilings and old lights with character. Hundreds of people filled the seats as well as the higher pews. Haley told me her dear friend Rachel and some of her sorority sisters were in the dance performance. This was to be the last night. As it started, I was surprised how much I enjoyed it as I knew a lot of the music. Haley told me so long as someone tried out they were accepted to the performance, regardless of their skill level.

In the first number the skill level was notably advanced. Next dance was clearly very new or first time dancers, who were carefully watching their every move, and yet their sheer courage and determination added to their dance performance and became riveting for me. Haley had two days earlier introduced me to a girl she lived with, yet did not get along with or "see eye to eye." When I heard she was in the dance I asked Haley to point her out as I was sure I would not recognize her amongst so many dancers. In the middle of the first half, I saw one particular dancer who stood out for me among the group. As the music played, this young dancer seemed to be in an altered state of pure bliss, joy and "the zone." Haley said that was the girl. I remarked I would not have known. She had apparently been dancing since age two, now twenty and it showed in her precision. What really moved me though was the unhappy person from days ago who was unfriendly even to me, was now truly transformed. She seemed to be flying and her face was bathed in light and joy. My daughter shared she had family rarely out to see her.

After the dance, I went to buy her a single rose from Haley and I. My daughter did not understand why, so I said because she was amazing in the dance and "kindness matters" even if she is unfriendly to you. With the hundreds of people, I was surprised how easy we found her. I said congratulations on an excellent and most exquisite dance from Haley and I. She said "Thank you," and I said "You have a true talent." She looked proud and yes, happy, "in her element." I said I have found on my own journey that when a person is doing what they love most, following their gift, their passion - that they shine and joy seems to radiate. She understood.

I felt like I was in the presence of the divine watching courageous dancers find their place perhaps for the first time being seen fully and transparently even in the rawness of their inexperience back dropped with decades long of dancers with feet of magic.

Total Cost: $10 play, $3 rose
Total Time: 8 minutes
Total Value: Priceless. It is very important to see people through new lenses each time you meet. Everyone, including myself, has good and bad days and personal challenges. Even if someone has in some way been unkind to you, the biggest gift you have to offer is sharing your kindness nonetheless.

ACTION 38

Yoga

Visiting my daughter, I was happy to accompany her to yoga class. I had taught Kundalini pregnancy yoga as a young woman and often missed it. As we set up our mats, my mat was borrowed, Haley's was brand new with tree etchings, I was aware of how full circle life was showing itself, i.e. kids sending me nature pictures, yoga with daughter who used to at 18 months sit on our dolphin rug attending my beloved Yogi Bhajan's classes. I remember Haley standing up and saying "Hello" and Yogi Bhajan saying it was okay although others were shushing her. He loved children and believed their presence in class- noise and all, was a part of his teachings.

As the teacher began, I was instantly relaxed by her words, "Trust your body's knowing how far to stretch." After an hour and ten minutes, we gathered our shoes and water. I asked Haley to give me a few minutes since I was a guest. I approached the teacher in her mid to late 30s to extend my thanks for a very relaxing and "restorative" class. She told me she by day was a financial analyst who recently got divorced - she had no kids, yet her dog was everything to her. She told me how her dream was to pay off her debts and teach yoga full-time. I told her I thought she would make an excellent teacher to the youth particularly in the college town, as her words were so motivating and supportive. She thanked me and hugged me.

Total Cost: 0
Total Time: 20 minutes
Total Value: Immeasurable. On any given day we cannot know the impact of our time, presence or kindness towards another human being. As busy as we all are, I have found, there is always time to share such acts of kindness.

ACTION 39

Cookies

Have you ever noticed how clean and tidy most outdoor parking lots are? Well, I do. I always see women pushing around their trash cans walking the inner and outer perimeters of the strip malls where I live.

On Friday, I sat parked and just observed the lady and her efforts. I got out of my car and brought her a bag of chocolate chip cookies and handed them to her. She looked at me questioningly and I said, "Here, these are really good cookies." She took the bag and I said, "Thank you for doing such a great job keeping the area so nice and clean." We smiled at each other and I saw her in my rear window sampling her goodies.

I often wonder if our parking lots were left for a few months "untouched" by these trash angels if then people would appreciate their contribution.

Total Cost: $1.00
Total Time: 5 minutes
Total Value: Priceless. Acknowledging another person is most certainly worth your

time and effort. Can you imagine if you pulled into a parking lot, if there was trash strewn everywhere, how would you feel?

ACTION 40

Ace

It is really important to listen thoroughly when you ask someone how they are doing. Kindness far extends our notion of gifts or monetary worth. I walked into my local Ace Hardware and as I was checking out, I asked the older female cashier "How is your day going?" Since no one was in line, she started telling me how her work day was. I really was present to listening to her short story. After she finished speaking, I simply said "Wow, sounds like a busy day and week. Seems to me you are really good at your job" and I smiled. She looked at me and said "Yes, I am" and beamed a big smile at me.

Total Cost: 0

Total Time: 3-4 minutes

Total Value: Priceless. Every person, regardless of their job status, where they live, how they look is worthy of your appreciation and therefore gratitude. Please consider this.

ACTION 41

Camping

Listening makes a difference and costs nothing. Sometimes I have found that asking people a question based on something they have shared is an important gesture of kindness. When my Thursday pool-man returned from his first family trip in ages, I went outside on a hot day to bring him a few otter pops and Gatorade.

I asked how his family camping trip was and he shared it was nice, yet they had encountered unexpected poor weather. He said he was not feeling well and I offered a vitamin C or Tylenol. He said "No, thank you," yet thanking me for remembering about his trip. He in turn asked me how my trip went with my Mom and husband, and I said "Great, yet, I always love returning home."

Total Cost: $1.25
Total Time: 4-6 minutes
Total Value: Priceless. Service people often go unnoticed, therefore stopping to inquire how they are doing has a big impact and is very much appreciated.

ACTION 42

Jell-O

Have you ever been in a store where you have heard someone ask where an item is, only to be told the number? Today, as I was checking out in a hurry to meet my gardener with a power cord, I heard an older woman ask "Where can I find boxed Jell-O?" reply - "Aisle 13." As I saw the lady's confused look I bee-lined to her and said, "Excuse me, ma'am, can I help you find your item?" She said "I want boxed Jell-O." I walked her to aisle 13 and pointed out the many flavors of gelatin.

I almost wanted to ask the young worker if perhaps she would show the customer the aisle, yet, decided I would be both, quicker and more patient doing it myself. As I left, running towards my car, I could not help but wonder why we do not naturally help each other out when we hear or see the call. In this case, Jell-O.

Total Cost: 0
Total Time: 2 minutes
Total Value: Immeasurable. Perhaps the senior lady felt relief or happiness about her

Jell-O. I am no different than anyone else, I have obligations, appointments, easy days and rough ones. Yet, what I do observe is kindness is my nature and I care so very much about sharing and helping people along the way.

ACTION 43

Wheels

Pulling up to the Chevron station I watched a man in his mid-50s wiping down his beautiful sports car. I saw other people admiring his beautiful wheels, yet, no one approached him. Kindness is not reserved only for the poor or any one group. I believe it is for every one of us!

I walked over to him and said, "Wow, sir, is that a pretty car." He beamed. I said my 15 ½ year old son would love it and we both spoke of boys and their love of cars. He said I could sit in it and take a picture. I said the picture would be great as both my son and husband would love his sports car. I took two pictures and he drove off.

While I appreciated the car's appeal, no part of me felt a need nor desire to sit in it, perhaps for also not wanting to in any way damage his pristine show car. The young men on the other side of the pump began speaking to me about cars. I said, "It sure was a beauty," and they said "Yes, likely in excess of $200,000!" I smiled and said I was content with my three year old Mazda. As we said goodbye I was keenly aware that kindness is all about open-hearted connection as the morning displayed.

Total Cost: 0
Total Time: 8-10 minutes
Total Value: Immeasurable. A connection with good people and complimenting a middle aged man on his treasured car earned me a big thank you from my son and husband upon seeing the photo.

ACTION 44

Grace

Driving 25 minutes north to a medical supply store on a breezy sunny day would not be my first choice. Yet, my husband located a sleep apnea mask so I agreed to go with him. Pulling in front of a strip-mall with electric wheelchairs brought me back in an instant to my son's snowboarding crash four years and four months ago- vivid associations of running on pure maternal adrenaline trying to locate him the best equipment.

As we entered the very congested store, I reminded myself Zach was okay now and how stores such as these had aided in his recovery. A lady named Emma greeted us with a huge smile. I instantly knew she was a very special person because her smile lit up the entire cramped store. As my husband tried on a few masks she and I joked and laughed about the Darth Vader quality of the sleep apnea masks. I asked her if she had kids and she told me she hoped and prayed for twins.

A young man appeared from the back, noticeably irritable, perhaps angry. She addressed him sweetly and asked if he could help the other people who just entered. He seemed either unaware or not connected to the presence of a disabled man with his family. She politely asked him again and he went over. I asked her if his energy affected her and she responded "Why would I want to carry that?" Before we left I reached over the counter and hugged this beam of sunshine named Emma. I whispered I would also pray for her to have twins.

Total Cost: 0
Total Time: 18-20 minutes
Total Value: Priceless. I saw how one lady in a dusty, dark and congested store could add sunshine with her smile.

ACTION 45

The Beach

Riley is my youngest child. He is a bright and giving person. When he gets picked up at the beach over the weekend by his Dad, they make a beeline for Taco Bell, Riley's main staple. His normal order consists of two plain burritos and an iced Mountain Dew slushie. In the beach areas, there are often many homeless people. Riley spotted an older man and asked Peter to get him some food and a drink, which he did. As Riley looked for him where he was moments earlier, he was not there - Riley was concerned that the man would be hungry and eventually gave the meal to another homeless person.

The next weekend as Peter was about to drop Riley and his friend off to the beach, he had a large bag: he said he packed peanut butter and jelly, cookies and drinks in case he saw another hungry person When my husband told me this I cried. Tears of beauty and gratitude that at 15 my son would care enough to do that. So you see, we are all capable to be kind towards each other and planting the seeds through example clearly works.

Total Cost: $4

Total Time: 20 minutes

Total Value: Priceless. To see one's own child spread acts of kindness unsolicited is a gift beyond measure. Please teach your own children through your own example of what you say and what you do.

ACTION 46

Hearts

It is 9am and I sit in the parking lot waiting for the walkers, cyclers, and workers to go in their many directions before quietly leaving my car. What is most interesting always to me is the people, all ages, shapes and sizes heading off left-right, North, South, East and West. I watch a city worker in his early 40s polishing the brass pieces at the entry point of Quail Trail Head. He carefully shines, polishes and rinses each piece in a quietly proud manner, inspecting his work closely. He neither looked up nor smiled yet, as I sit 20 feet away, I can feel his efficiency, his strong work ethic. He takes his time and I notice his proud posture as he returns to his sports utility vehicle that is clean and respectful looking, much like he appears.

A couple in their late 30s stretches at the benches leading to the trail and I see he is holding a recyclable, environmentally safe large water bottle. I wonder if they have known each other long as they seem at ease, yet indifferent. A group of four-five women cyclists appear in the parking lot returning from a bike trek, it is already quickly warming up at 76° and they excitedly talk in loud-animated voices. As they load their bright colored bikes I am aware of wanting to be a part of their group, even just for a few moments as their energy is contagious. A photographer with a huge camera and tripod scopes the areas - the wild flowers are beginning to really peek out from their slumber and the bright orange California poppies are scattering in small amounts. By May, everywhere you look in Southern California you will be greeted by these dainty, yet vibrant bursts of nature's glory.

It is now been 40 minutes and I see the path is clear aside from the photographer who keeps re-appearing in the shrubbery. I walk to the entry of the path 20 feet or so from where I am parked and survey the land: my main objective is to spread a bit of love and magic for people, yet I wish to do so as anonymously as possible to keep it about the message of love. I grab my water bottle, stick and two mini sparkles bottles. The ground is in partial shade at the opening so drawing the heart is fairly easy to do. I tell myself, I must work quickly before the next group appears or the hikers complete the 1.8 mile loop. I choose pink sparkles and fill the center and edges with glitter: it is virtually impossible not to smile and I begin to laugh in joy just seeing the pale pink sparkles dance in the sandy dirt. I jog to the other end of the path and it is noticeably hotter and impossible for me to draw another heart, so I empty the entire contents of my eight ounce water bottle and draw a larger heart. I sprinkle with so much love that the pale green sparkles and my heart feels light and bright and hopeful on this beautiful-sunny Friday morning. Perhaps seeing these two hearts will lift the spirits of someone in need.

I jog to my car with a gentle, sweet grace filling my being: I care so very much about people and yes, I want them to know they matter and things can and will get better. As I drive down Sand Canyon to go about my day, I am struck by how little it takes to make a difference and how yet that gesture can maybe help, support, inspire and uplift even one human being, it is worth the effort completely. The wheels in my heart's soul engine start churning and ideas for the next day's love-inspired message fill me with enthusiasm and joy.

Total Cost: $2
Total Time: 45 minutes
Total Value: Immeasurable. Even if one person walking, biking or jogging on a trail who faces a challenge or has had a rough day, now feels lighter and brighter for having seen the magical heart, it was well worth the effort.

ACTION 47

Dirt

Wow, it is unbelievable how warm yet magnificent 64° can seem when you are staring out at such a vast landscape: I am lucky to get the last parking spot out of perhaps 15, as the early morning health conscious individuals aspire to avoid the noon-day sun. I carefully approach the path's opening and quickly get busy drawing a heart with a jagged rock - in a moment I am jarred by two dirt bike riders approaching me fast that I neither heard nor saw. I walk to the parking lot and remove my lightweight jacket.

Speaking to the athletic man next to my car, I share with him my simplistic vision: to inspire, uplift and support people through loving gestures in the dirt. He pauses and says, "Yes people do not look up often or connect," which is why for now I write messages in the dirt. We say goodbye and that gives me another idea: what about just standing one day and saying "Great job" or "I see you." Onwards I go, in such gratitude.

Total Cost: 0
Total Time: 6 minutes

Total Value: Immeasurable. We often do not know the weight of one small act of kindness on another person's, perhaps heavy heart. I invite you to consider in which ways you, too can offer your kindness to others.

Epilogue

Impact

We can never know for certain how showing up for others in words, time, presence, actions or gifts can impact their lives for the better. Sometimes, as I have found, it is as simple as a person feeling seen and appreciated. Other times, the impact can be far greater. I have shared with you some of the letters written to me and also sent to the Ellen DeGeneres "Nominate a Powerful Woman Who Has Impacted the Lives of Others" contest. I appreciate the numerous letters that were written to Ellen in appreciation for my life's work on "Kindness on a Budget." While I am a simple and private woman, it would be a great honor to have a larger platform in which to spread the message of kindness. It is my deepest heartfelt wish that some of the stories, that are all true, have perhaps inspired you to share more freely in your daily lives. The letters you read are all 100% real, and I have kept the identity of the authors' private, due the sensitive nature of the content.

In gratitude and love,
Suzie "Harijot" Abels, M.S.

Letters

1) I know a few people who have genuinely changed someone's life; I know even fewer who have genuinely changed many people's lives. But I know only one who lives and breathes to make those around her — family and strangers alike — more hopeful. Her name is Suzie Abels and, when she's not running after her three exceedingly difficult children (this author being one of them), she is busy innovating new ways to restore hope in the downtrodden. She's basically an entrepreneur of the soul. I see Suzie's footprint on this world as a series of spontaneous, small acts of kindness — the kind of little gestures most people would mistakenly dismiss as frivolous. I mean, how many you know would drive around the neighborhood handing out ice-cold Gatorades to the city workers breaking their backs to fill pot-holes and trim trees in the sweltering summer heat? Cash-flushed though she certainly is not, Suzie has an incredible ability to identify the smallest gestures that would make the biggest impact in somebody's day. So, what does this have to do with changing lives? There is nothing in this world as powerful as restoring someone's faith in humanity. It is far too easy to focus only on one's own hardships and ignore the suffering of others. Suzie transmits selflessness and kindness to nearly everyone she meets, and to contagious effect. We live in an unspeakably self-interested world.

Suzie is bringing empathy back into fashion and asks for nothing in return.

2) I would like to tell you about a most unique person, Suzie Abels. Suzie has a gift which impacts everyone she encounters; from close friends to total strangers she just meets on the street. Her ability to soothe, interpret and provide intuitive and spiritual insights about people and their lives is special and something that is not taught, developed or gained from others. I have known Suzie for many years and when I was going through some extremely difficult challenges a few years ago, including a near catastrophic accident that happened to my daughter, Suzie provided me with guidance, wisdom and insights that enabled me to accept what was happening and deal with the circumstances with a very calming mindset. Her ability to cut through the b.s. and touch your soul is truly admirable. Her twitter posts on @IntuitiveSuzie are thought provoking and perceptive. After spending five minutes speaking with you, Suzie's kind and thoughtful demeanor elevates one's spirit to a level many of us never thought we could achieve. I believe that fans and viewers of Ellen would experience her gentle yet powerful impact and encourage you to further research her special "talents."

3) For the last 10 months what I've needed was a nurturing steady stream of love and kindness when my sister passed last October. One woman stepped into my world to be that very presence; listening, comforting reassuring gently. Tokens would arrive in the mail as cards charms bracelets stuff animals. Texts emails and messages of prayer and support have streamed forth from this incredible woman. Through the closely following passing of my mother and then uncle

Through the array of travels ceremonies and legal matters to face address and navigate through this strong and constant presence of loving kindness from the other side of the country from a person who new me only because of her relationship with another has been a healing life line for me through the simplest moments. A committed soul a clear and conscious being has been riding this wave of life with me. I don't know how she's always known how to be how she is in her whole life and in mine. I only know I am so incredibly grateful she has and is.

4) Suzie is a powerful, intuitive and compassionate Woman, who lights up every room she enters. There is no one in this World who has a bigger heart or a greater ability to heal the souls of the people with whom she has contact. When I was 38, I underwent surgery. Suzie was able to absorb all of my physical pain and emotional anguish. Suzie allowed me to heal by tapping into my own positive energy. She did this with her ability to make me laugh, even in the worst moments, at doctors' appointments and post-surgery. When Suzie decides that something is going to happen, she makes it happen. There is no stopping her! When Suzie decides you are going to love her, there just is no option and love her you will! Suzie is an excellent bargain hunter and she stock piles clothing and household items so that when she comes across people in need, she has the ability help. When Suzie noticed that the pool guy was wearing torn sneakers, she bought him new shoes. Suzie regularly runs out of the house with cold drinks for the association landscapers working down the street in the hot sun. We rarely use a housekeeper, but recently when we did, she insisted that they took a break and sat down to rest and eat a snack. There is no kinder person in this World than Suzie Abels! Suzie has also created a secret garden that has transformed the lives of people who visit. Suzie's kindness is an inspiration and she touches people's hearts every day.

5) Suzie Abels is a woman with a beautiful spirit who spends her days amplifying the wonderful joy that resides in all of us. She helps make as many people possible feel loved through simple acts of kindness. Her book, "Kindness On a Budget" focuses on opening others to the many possible ACTIONs of helping make anyone's day better through easy-to-do, budget conscious, and many times free ways. Suzie is a strong woman who inspires those around her to want happier lives for themselves by bringing happiness to others' lives. By doing things such as creating our Joyous Garden at a viewpoint near her home, she has influenced her community in a positive way. The last few years the garden has become a place for people from various backgrounds to come and find peace; a safe and serene hill for people to clear their minds and contemplate life. Suzie's impact on the lives of those in the area is made evident through the journal entries written at the hill by those who view the garden as their own happy place. Along with being an author who cares about all people, Suzie is a healer, life coach, loving mother and wife. Every person lives a unique life by deciding what one wants to spend their time doing. Suzie made the decision to dedicate her life to understanding how people can achieve lasting joy and be freed from negative experiences that hold them back. With her guidance many people have been able to believe in themselves and the world around them once again. Lights amplify one another.

6)   Suzie is a powerful woman with a global mission: her purpose is to spread a simple formula that reaches the hearts and minds of people all over the world: it is that KINDNESS MATTERS!

Suzie is a living example of her devotion: she spreads light and love every day, in so many ways. Often she chooses to remain anonymous in her generosity; creating a hilltop 'secret garden' with plants, a book for sharing inspiration and lovingly placed tokens: designed to create sacred space for all who come here. This project has blossomed into a small community project that involves young people. Instead of leaving behind broken glass and destruction, they now feel responsible for the maintenance of the secret garden and take good care of it.

Suzie also loves to send out notes to others, handwritten and decorated. In those she might include a generous gift, just for the sheer joy of sharing. In addition to offering her healing work to those who seek her out, she supports many causes actively. Suzie demonstrates every day that KINDNESS MATTERS, thus setting an example for others to follow. Her light shines brightly into a world that needs kindness more than ever.

"Bless be the ones who serve others. They are the ones who find heaven on earth."

Yogi Bhajan

CPSIA information can be obtained
at www.ICGtesting.com
Printed in the USA
FSOW04n0213290915
11523FS